The wo

CAITLIN SAUNDERS

Love is not what you say, it is what you do.

First edition
Printed December 2020

ISBN: 978-1-5272-7969-8

Contents

Notes

This collection covers a three-year period in my early twenties, from September 2017 to September 2020. During that time, my life was consumed by unprocessed trauma and a desperate need for safety—something which I felt only romantic love could offer. I dedicated myself to a relationship which felt like my greatest love but was the longest act of self-destruction I had ever embarked on.

Many of the poems in this book were written as love poems. Many of these love poems normalise doubt, manipulation, and self-deception. When I wrote them, I was frightened of being alone. This fear drove me to ignore my instincts for self-protection. My partner could then convince me that having basic emotional needs made me unlovable. I became dependent on the warmth and security I felt in our relationship, even between the storms of arguments, infidelity, and manipulation.

I am sharing this collection because I think it is vital that we eradicate shame around loneliness and romantic pain. Throughout my early twenties, I have wanted to feel loved more than I have cared about anything else. It was only when the love I had longed for, and worked tirelessly to retain, left me with a shell of a life (and almost without a life at all) that I faced my shame and asked why.

This book is not a cautionary tale against compromise or trust, but an account of how the wounded can be deceived and deceive ourselves, until we are ultimately wounded again. It has no neat, happy ending, but its existence is itself a step towards healing.

I.

Before

Baiting

Baiting. A falconry term.
I am handler and handled.
She is the reason I am here,
But she is wild.

I hold her up.
Calm breaths, arm aching.
A rustle, prickle. I see it
Just before she baits. Desperate, crazed.

The source of fear unseen.
What makes me love her,
Her thick life, detail, keen eye.
When she baits, I hate it all.

Come back, wild messy thing.
Sit still once again.
Ignore your fears, pathologies,
They are wrong.

Do as I say,
Follow my rule.
Let me protect you.
Your feelings are not true.

Onto Mill Road

Short-sleeves and shorts green,
Down onto Mill Road. On two wheels
And across from my window.
There is a woman who you try
To overtake. But no,
You have taken over enough girls
For today.

The next ten minutes, few hours,
Two days: Where were you going?
Do you have a place, a person, that way?
I pass over cobbles, through history,
On two wheels. A car screeches,
Someone shouts. I am a wound,
Unhealed.

What is it about your 7 months—
7 from 282—that make me undo?
It is an answer I already know:
You listened, caught me, were warm,
And then let go.
I wish there were more of your things
I could burn or throw.

You never really said a sentence that
I was interested to hear.
Average intelligence, looks, education, desires.
You painted yourself as an empty bowl
Into which I could pour all my fear.
You volunteered to tame a wild tiger,
Blindfolded. Stupid.

—An interlude—
I need more anxiety pills.
Can you tell me why?
Well, I had a boyfriend who used
To rape me. And then I had a new
Boyfriend who was looking after me. But then
I told him what happened, and he left me,
And I'm all alone and it's scary.
Say that
But with a throat full of tears.
The poor student doctor looked away,
Closed up her ears.

It's nobody's fault; you did your best.
It's not like you were the only one to fail my test.
The unbearable part, what makes me cry on my bike
And hold up my shields,
Is how you never said sorry. You left me to hold in
My own blood, my own spilling guts.

There are days, weeks, months,
When I bleed out. Mind finally clear
Of you. But then,
There you are, cycling down
Onto Mill Road.
Short-sleeves and shorts green,
Right past my window.

Fathers

Do you know the weirdest part?
Seeing your dad.
Cycling, walking the dog, testing his car.
A connection so uncomfortable, weak,
Unexpressed in lyrics or art.

And I know he recognises me.
His shoulders locked, squinting eyes,
His masked fright. Why?
I imagine his thoughts must be something like:

'What hurt did my son pass to you?
Girl I met in the kitchen,
Eyes big with love after so few months.
My wife still speaks your name in hope.'

But maybe that is not why he's wary.
Maybe the tears I shed on his doorstep were objectively
 scary.
'I'm glad my boy is free of your grasp.
I'll fund his crawl across the globe for as long as this
 lasts—
For as long as it takes for you to let go.'

Here is just another question, unanswered:
Sons and their fathers.
Like the other one; no hair on his crown,
Neither able to speak of love without a frown.

I don't want that, it's not for me.
Give me a man. Singular. Free.

Red circle

My mind is a sneaking thing.
With so much conviction,
I do not want you.
Shan't.

Red circle. Fluttering heart.
I want someone to love me
Because, for all that I say,
I can't.

Why do I only ever want to open
The boxes without seals?
Not a zip or a fold.
No entry, no fun.

"You deserve someone who
Wants to make you happy."
Such a soft buzz,
An impossible one.

Slow motion car crash.
How can I ever be serious?
Crazy, maddening little girl.
The messy friend.

I cup my hands, open-mouthed,
To catch the hurts boys pour out.
Thinking: 'This is it.
It could be love in the end.'

II.

Fall

G

"So will this make it
Into the journal?"
It doesn't need to,
I'll never forget it.

You are not a flame or wisp of smoke
Slipping my grasp,
But the hissing stream
Of air from a puncture, squeezed.

Present only on a hovering palm
And in the rushing sink
As the sound meets my ears.
I resist. No.

It is too much like letting go
Of the twisting hose,
So newly caught. You don't know
How much you scare me.

Clutter is everywhere: my evenings, feelings,
Shoulders, mind.
Your blue crates, bursting with a life
So completely not mine.

I can't run this fast, this path,
Forever. But neither
Can I hold still a single night.

You make the journal,
'The cut'.

And you make me grin,
Make me twist my gut.

Can I do a test?
Try before you buy.
Is it because or in spite of you
That I cry?

My life

Why is there no happy centre
To this clawed thing?
No calm, still middle
In the pendulum swing.

It's just, I thought you said—
Ghosts of 'should be'—
Either respect for you
Or breathing for me.

I unfold issues in a crooked room;
Green carpet and a clock
I cannot see.
This isn't my life.

I flounder, trip, rise;
Hunched shoulders and aching neck.
Your light eyes and thick thumbs
Make my disaster into a speck.

I'm sorry I hate myself.
I'm confused that you don't.
This ticking, this buzz, cannot be
Stopped, only slowed.

It

It feels
Like there was no one
Before you. My breath
Squeezed, skin prickling raw.
When you are with me,
Baby—chest, shoulder and skin
—Your smell
Is everywhere.

Why do you think I
So love to push my nose to your neck?
When we stand together, still.
It smells of our nights
(And our mornings);
A world with nothing but
You in (me).

It feels
Like I can never push
Against your palms enough.
Like there is no life
Beyond your tongue.
Like my hips are empty
Without you there,
Filling the hot air.

Taking it well

What did you eat? Taste?
A burger, popcorn?
Her cunt, her lips?

It's the pressure of a question.
So I am jogging, reading,
Texting. Looking elsewhere.

Like you did, but not.
"3km. Let's just go somewhere."
You had it. Took it all.

He. That would sound better,
To draw a line.
But 4 weeks is nothing.
That 'he' was mine.

Work in progress

The dips and squeezes of me,
This rolling wave of antipathy, does not
Disappear but can get faded, hazy,
In the no-smell of your shoulder.

Cliché 1: blue eyes, bright
2: soft hair and skin
3: the shape of your words—voice
And 4? Short glances and grins

We have tried trying
(And lying and crying and
Broken trust).
You hitch-hiked to me with a mangled clutch.

You are everything my teen self
Did not want.
My push back with both hands
Against her anger and mistrust.

To me you are a crossword,
Upside down. And it has taken time
To see that the answers
Are also that way around.

Doubt

Little pockets of doubt open,
Like pulled or missed stitches
In our seam.
The way you answer:
That tugged frown.

Insecurities, self-hate, gape
Like wounds spread wide
On my crown.
Friend of a friend;
Voice through a window.

Eternal sunshine of the spotless mind.
What I would give to wipe clean,
To breathe free.
Spirit in my cuts,
'Kerchief on my cheek.

You hold me when I shake,
Soothe when I cry.
I don't want that—
I want still limbs,
I want dry eyes.

A heavy sickness tightens
Like long fingers or thread
Around my insides.
This isn't me,
This lot will not always be mine.

AZ

Quiet and a little dim,
A cove of my own.
But all blue-check: yours,
Even the shirt collar around my neck.

I know how to block, defend,
Dislike. Not this dreidel
Of love and rage.
I have felt alone for an age.

Space, respect, a tip-toe.
These define my family's life
And it takes a lot to be
The someone else that you want.

I am small, with adulthood
As my walls. And you,
My grown up, acting the child.
A safety blanket, gone.

Why can I not be sad?
You are so quick to temper,
Our arguments land like stones
And float like feathers.

(Am I looking for issues?
Am I justified?
I'm scared)

AZ #2

An open, light brightness
High and empty air.
Where are the broken stones,
The out of place hairs?

There is so much silence, still,
On this clean table, bare.
It has all the makings of a fresh start;
Of water unrippled, like glass.

If this is your home then I
Think that I know why my
Mess and darkness and hairline cracks
Pull at your senses and known facts.

Everything here is spikey, out to hurt,
And the colours and lines are soft
But not blurred. AZ, I swear I see
That you have more than 100 years.

Your rocks and dust and dry heat
All feel much more like true history,
Than my golden buildings
And halls of candles and cheese.

I long for more of your pale dirt
Between my toes, under feet.
America has taken this place of harsh life
And turned it into human paradise.

47 minute train

I miss him so often,
Like waves on a shore
Each time reaching higher
And pulling back more.

I view myself so seriously
But he is a game,
And the time taken to see this
Is my biggest shame.

I mix my 'want' with 'deserve'
Despite frequent dips to my own depths and pools.
When he 'desires', I hear 'requires', and prove
That my distributaries are clouded and crude.

I wish I could paint or draw or sculpt
So I could show you the joys of his face.
I once wanted dark hair, heavy brow,
But now, his blond is what makes me race.

Dear GPT

Dear GPT,
How do I feel about you?
You fill my whole arms,
Stomach and head.
My heart and chest.
I know your shape and don't,
You are everything
And yet barely there–
So familiar; safe.

But you can rip open fear
With the smallest words.
Don't let this keep you from
Being true, because losing you
Would be like dropping my
New phone.
I would cry and kick and scream
And grieve my empty hands.
But afterwards, I would still be me.

GPT, your company shows me
That I am stronger than I
Thought, and less often correct.
My stubborn 'emotional insight'
Drives you a bit crazy.
Your focused frown, sudden smile,
And strong hands, melt me.
You know just how to hold.
The right way to smell.

You are a book: "Read me," you beg.

Thirty short stories, a limerick,
A lot of politics.
But those chapters at your heart?
Glued shut. Me, scared to pull
Too hard.
Here, we mismatch; I pour out
Pain and can't say back my fun.
A difference, perhaps, for the best?

It is starting to show that we
Do not fit like ying and yang,
Like puzzle pieces or a hand in a hand.
We fit like puppies asleep,
All over each other in a warm heap.
In this life we will squeak and wriggle
And shove but, if we wake,
We won't bite, just
Lick each other's scruff.

III.

Break

Doorway

Say something to her.
She is in the doorway, quiet,
Back from where you sent her
So you could chase a man
Who told you she was not real.
Say something!
Tell her how her hair has grown,
How warm it was between storms.
Do not apologise, it's okay;
She is no longer a child.

Ask her for a hug, a glass of wine.
Look at her, really do, and
She will look, truly, at you.
This time it is not like before,
And it shows. You will keep the photos,
You will keep the adventures and pride.
She has grown in your absence:
A caterpillar, cocooned, now flies.

Is softness a weakness?
You ask the stars. But she is here
And will tell you, "In part."
If only when you cushion the fall
For someone who tore you up by video call.
For a person who pushed you to be someone else,
For one who asked you to quell yourself.
She is real, she is here, going nowhere.
As many times as you leave her, she will be there.
Say something to her. Tell her you care.

Romance

Am I a romantic,
Or just an idiot?
'Just' as if there is a difference
Between foolish and fool.
Between closing my eyes when walking
A cliff, and letting nights that broke me
Be a 'lovers' tiff'.

Is romance dead? Or is it only
Misunderstood—Because sitting pretty
For your sexist friends
Must mean things with us are good.
Waiting and cleaning and apologising
For feeling. This is love, pure and true,
And all. About. You.

Afterwards

Standing still in a wooded glade,
Sheltering from the rain with
Cambridge United perfectly framed
By wet leaves,
I cry and cry, and pause
For the passing of a cyclist.

This little patch of trees
Is a shithole and
This pathetic shower—misty, thin—
Feels like a metaphor for my
Slow-motion, clinging hurt.
For how the unworthy and small
Has pulled apart my all.

If I had a breath of certainty
In income or in home, then I might
Rejoice at being alone because a smile
Cannot outweigh the pressure of
Never passing the changing goalposts of your love.

But as it is, what do I have to grasp?
Where should I be?
Why do I want no friend
But only you, in this,
To hold and calm me?

Green Earth

Would Sir Attenborough be disappointed
At the energy I waste on you?
Tissue after tissue after tissue.
Bedside lamp burning, Instagram whirring,
I wish I could shut my eyes and think of the penguins.

Love, fear, heartbreak and tears
—As natural as can be, we say:
'It's not life without a little loss!'
But there will be nothing left on green Earth
With me leaking and weeping to another pillow wash.

I hope dear David forgives me
For how many hours of light
I use to reshare empowering quotes.
And for all the paper pages I have filled
With letters I will never send to you.

Cake

I feel like a tin
With the cake scraped out.
My walls, grey, remain
But inside will never
Be quite the same.

There are some crumbs,
A smear of icing on my face,
And in the corners, I suppose,
Those hard, brown-baked bits
(Which were always my favourites).

What was I before?
Victoria sponge, coffee, carrot cake?
I don't know. I baked for so long
Without tasting and he ate,
Then left without waiting.

My choice will always be traybake
With red jam and coconut flakes.
Maybe that is what I'll be,
Shaped and flavoured just for me
(Finally).

In trouble

I have not told a soul
What we did. It hasn't
Passed my lips. And as
Time slips away, I know
That I won't until
The heartache is gone.

Words in grey and green did
Escape my fingertips, but
What are pixels from friends afar
Next to girls with wine and
Cigarettes? And cruel cracks of
How much fitter I am than you.

I said that day and
Every since; no one knows
But you what is lost.
And yet, it is only you
I am not to speak to.
Your hands felt good.

So fitting to end how it began:
Rush and promise,
The same sleeping sheets.
I have not told a soul
What we did; what I found
In eyes, smile, hips.

IV.

Space

Staple Island

On that tiny island, that 'spit of land',
Stained yellow and white with mess and lichen,
I watched the puffins hum overhead
To sea and back, fish and back. Back.
The freedom of air and sea and wilderness
Is monotony. Is food, young, food, young.
What sonnets might a puffin pen
If for a 9-to-5 and a microwave meal?

Would my sorrows melt were I only
To Fly to sea and back, fish and back?
I ask because puffins do not care about read receipts.
I can surely blame my laze for this because I learnt it
With him. Have you noticed how close they are?
Idle and idyll. And idleness in love is idyllic but
When those golden shores disappear, our hours
Gape with their absence. Idle despair.

This pocket place has rock, sea, sun, and rain.
A world unto its own where life is clear.
Salt and fish in the air turns to knots in my hair
But this bliss of waves and wet moss cannot
Chase off my pain how woodland and childish games
Once could. I walk to shore and back,
'Fish' and back, but the freedom is monotony.
I could not compete with our puffin poets
But I can feel sorrier for myself than them.

8th June

Pink linen on pink skin
Flutters in the North Atlantic Ocean wind.
White weave hat flops
This way and that as she gesticulates,
Wildly, to herself and the birds
Asking the Heavens their names.

It is so blue—So *blues*—
Because there are shades upon some,
Stretching away, marking the depth
Of the waters and whiteness
Of the clouds. Even the mountains have been
Made blue by distance and
The intervening cerulean sky.

She came here for nothingness;
To tan and think and not cry.
But she found volcanic rock, black as night
And a glimpse into paradise.
She found dinner alone, the perfect Spanish tone.
She found a bench on the promenade
At 9pm, watched the sun set,
And said, "Thank you" again and again.

Start of September

The deep peace of evening river stroll,
In the dying sun as London burns.

The soft joy of warm beer in grass,
Sips, as people chant.

Should I be scared? Angry?
None are not, but me.

Here: river walks and beer.
In slow-motion,
All our disasters and fear.

V.

Reignition

Wish

If I could have one wish,
It would be not to love you.

I drag myself through days
And separate from friends to hear
You say down the phone that
You want me back. Down *my* call.
And then to watch the grey
Tick age and decay as you pretend
I am not there until our date,
Which you change. Because you
Can always rearrange me.
The girl whose trust you're 'earning'.
The girl whose heart and two-
To-three years you're burning.

If I could have one wish,
It would be not to love you.

Floral sheets

Soft curve, a freckle on your back.
There is warmth here and after
A week of emotions' deepest throes
I want to sign the dotted line
To say that you are mine.

The most humbling is to look
At your feet and the hair at
Your ankles because it reminds me
That you are a big, grown person
Committed to my smiles and safety.

These moments when I watch you breathe
And when you sleepily squeeze my body
Are our purest intimacy. But are they
True? Because my words hurt you and
Your eyes do drift away. We fight.

We live outside—around?—a knot and
We watch as it flops to us each,
Then away. Neither knows what to say
Or even if and how and what we want.

I hope the answer is your bare chest
Under my cheek at night.

Small garden

Small garden in May morning sun.
Your wooden deck and a black coffee
(If I close my eyes), can make you
Madrid, or Rome. Or Lanzarote.

The wood pigeon's coo gives us away,
But that's okay. I am somewhere exotic
But closer to home...
Brighton. Mid Wales. The Norfolk Coast.

Small garden, you are my world,
And you are as good as the world.
You, your mirror out front,
And the red cube of rooms between.

You saw me make S'mores with the love of my life.
Cry chasing pets in the rain.
We fixed the rosebush, did sit-ups,
And together, we even had honeybees.

Small garden in May morning sun,
You are as good as the world.

Our short stint

Cooking late, cheese sauce,
Legs crossed on the sofa
Going over how you shouldn't drink port.

Shooting through the window,
Around doors. Paint chip,
My forfeit, with knees at my ears.

These are the things we did,
The things I will miss.
This was our short stint.

Hot tub in the cold.
Bums, chests, your hold
Too close on my side of the bed.

Dancing in the living room,
Tequila before wine.
Deep kisses, spinning; you were mine.

3pm break, then suddenly it's 8.
We had two big fights
And endless nights intwined.

Afternoon beer bongs,
Did even that feel wrong?
I thought this was our beginning,
Not our end.

VI.

Disgrace

Scooped out

All the poems in me have been scooped out.
Last time, you ate my cake.
This time, you scraped out my ice cream
And threw the cold, empty tub away.
(You never did know how to recycle)

From the smoke and wreckage of
Yet another hurricane-shaped-like-you,
I am pulling my broken pieces.
Stringing them together to try to build a life.
(I have lived in four houses in one year)

How do you make jumping from a cliff
Feel like flying? Feel free?
How do you make your rot, your decay,
Taste fresh and sweet?
(Nothing you owned was ever clean)

You didn't earn my trust but took it anyway.
Didn't share my love but asked me to stay.
Don't want my words so I give them away.

Infections

Are you prone to infections?
Not the kind she means.
Infectious yawn? Check. Laugh? Yes.
But what about
Contemplating your own death?

The men I had these past years
Were like ink on wet paper.
They spread into the pattern of my veins,
Crossed over; mixed. Blue, red, green becoming black.
So heavy that I tore and stained.

My defences, immune system, are worn.
Thin, as if my inside is an empty shell.
They were not diseases or colds,
Just square pegs trying
To fit a round hole.

I have been used, and made a fool,
One, two, five, seven times.
Each alone—what? A cough? A sneeze?
But together, almost the end of me.

An island

They say no man is an island, but this woman is.
Each time I tune my radio or let lighthouses blare,
I am raided; my land trampled and desecrated.
How and who should I be cultivating?
Others wish only to plant their own seed.

I do not know who I am unpainted by another
But the beginning is not a blank slate.
Behind the mirror is a void, one which has swallowed
 for too long.
It has grown a beast in me, held by growing walls
—An island paradise, where she can roar.

About the writer

Caitlin grew up in Cwmbran, South Wales. In 2013, she moved to Cambridge for university and studied linguistics. Caitlin remained in Cambridge, working for the university, after graduating in 2017. She made new friends, hosted a radio show on CamFM 97.2, and enjoyed weekends and evenings in the city's pubs and cafés.

Much of this collection was written while Caitlin was living in Cambridge with friends. It was completed when she was living in Bury St Edmunds with her ex-partner. In July 2020, Caitlin and her three guinea pigs relocated to her parents' home in Goytre, Monmouthshire. This book was self-published there, in what Caitlin describes as 'an effort to make something positive from a long and difficult period'.

Caitlin hopes to write more in the future.

Acknowledgements

Thank you to Ellie and Celia, for loving me even when I couldn't love myself. Thank you to my mum for driving over 200 miles to give me a hug. Thank you to Kara and Anna for your wisdom, your wit, and for all the alcohol. Thank you to Sam for always being there. Thank you to Rémy, Jenny, David, Elly, Alex, and Emma for the different ways you have always shown that you care.

Thank you to my brothers, Dylan and Tom, for giving so much of your time to this project. Dylan, your photographs will always be central to this collection for me. Tom, your encouragement gave me the confidence to share these poems with the world.

Thank you to everyone whose donations made this book possible.

Qasim Alli	Nick Matthews
Jade Aubrey	Alexander Mayes
Ellie Bishop	Elle McCluskey
Joanna Drury	Celia Morris
Emma Flint	Leah Moss
Sarah Flint	Paul Pattison
David Goulding	Chloe Pritchard
Alison Green	Tom Saunders
Joseph Gregory	Dylan Saunders
Sam Holloway	Mark Saunders
Chelé Howard	Alison Saunders
Elly Humphrey	Kitty Saunders
Viv James	Kathryn Singleton
Louise King	Jo Ward
Jenny Lomax	
Hollie Marshall